In Between
Angels and Animals

'just as Dante divines:
we hover in between
angels and animals'

– 'Ode to Lost Poems', p. 50

Emily Cullen

IN BETWEEN
ANGELS AND ANIMALS

ARLEN
HOUSE

IN BETWEEN ANGELS AND ANIMALS

is published in 2013 by
ARLEN HOUSE
42 Grange Abbey Road
Baldoyle,
Dublin 13,
Ireland
Phone/Fax: 353–86–8207617
Email: arlenhouse@gmail.com
arlenhouse.blogspot.com

978–1–85132–079–0, paperback

Distributed internationally by
SYRACUSE UNIVERSITY PRESS
621 Skytop Road, Suite 110
Syracuse, NY 13244–5290, USA
Phone: 315–443–5534/Fax: 315–443–5545
Email: supress@syr.edu

Typesetting ¦ Arlen House
Printing ¦ Brunswick Press

CONTENTS

ACKNOWLEDGEMENTS

Grateful acknowledgements are due to the editors of the publications where some of these poems originally appeared: *The Burning Bush, The Black Mountain Review, Crannóg* (numbers 13, 17 & 21), *Carty's Poetry Journal, Divas! New Irish Women's Writing, Microphone On: Poetry from the White House Pub Limerick, Ireland, Go NUIGE Seo I & II, The Galway Advertiser, Light Falls* anthology of the DLS Literary Society 2012, *The Galway Review* Issue 1, Spring 2013 and *The Burning Bush II.* The poem 'Primavera' was selected as 'Poem of the Week' by the Australian Poetry organization and first published on its website (www.australianpoetry.org) and in its journal, *Sotto,* in September 2012. I would like to thank my parents, Cyril and Margie Cullen, and my sisters, Benita, Tara and Margot for all their love and encouragement. Thank you also to my sister Margot for her original art work. I want to express my gratitude to my dear friend, Pat Jourdan and to Philip Salom for valuable feedback and support.

For my husband, Kevin
and son, Lee
with all my love and gratitude

IN BETWEEN ANGELS AND ANIMALS

EMBODIMENT

i Maternal

I lie on the bed in darkness,
wary of sudden toddler jerks
(your innocent, erratic strength).
Instead, you lay your head upon my cheek,
and in that momentary tenderness,
[is] a universe of visceral wisdom.
I am held by this intuition:
love
free of all condition.

ii Marital

We grasp each other.
Words surrender
to spoor of pore.
You kiss my collarbone.
Sacred contours
underscore
quibbles and stresses.
Our limbs recall
a geography
of catharsis;
the lee of my back,
the lie of your land.

NIGHT OWLS

Like a spacehopper on its side,
inflated to air-capacity,
I struggle to recall
where is safe to lay
my eighth-month bulge.

Did she say turn left or right?
Afraid to roll onto my front,
encumbered with heartburn,
strained bladder, pins
and needles; each stage
shatters sleep.

Before dawn I take
a restful bath,
like Archimedes,
displace my weight;
I am now the breadth
of a beached whale.

But I am redeemed,
an insomnia queen,
dab hand at displacement.
I marshal marauding thoughts,
into useful to-do lists.

All the while,
you keep me company
with your soft, glorious kicking,
auguring we will share
circadian rhythms.

LOVE AND MILK

My breasts wake me up.
Tingling fullness
coaxes me onto my back.
Like the miracle of the loaves and fishes
my night supply has been replenished.
In my thirty-sixth year
my body has learned a new skill.

Your head jerks,
eyes brighten
as you spot my nipple.
Fists clench, unfurl,
fingers curl round my thumb.
Hidden tunnels carry milk:
aquaducts bearing fresh water
to a Roman fountain.

How should I cope with my cornucopia?
When you suckle one side
the other leaks.
'Each drop is precious', they say
so I also express for the rainy day.

Mouthing wide rhythms,
you reach the hind milk.
I tickle your toes to keep you awake
but it's you who lulls me to doze.

We've come a long way here
from sore cracks and Lanolin cream.
By the time you've drawn out your feed
we're ready to curl up side by side,
drift into a mutual nap
make up for a night without sleep.

A PROMENADE

Clare looks far away today;
hills portend rain.
I'm a centaur with wheels
instead of hooves,
propelled by gales –
not quite the *flaneuse;*
a shadow pushing a pram
past Mutton Island.
Behind me: the Prom.

Briny onslaught takes my breath,
jolts me out of sluggishness.
Hair flaps against my cheeks.
I am an elongated figure
like a Jack Yeats,
but do I still qualify
as a 'woman of destiny'?
Or am I an invisible mother
pushing a buggy into the sea?

I walk towards the Claddagh
into the miasma
of a divided sky
where I encounter
Louis MacNeice's lines,
etch his words upon
an afternoon slipping away,
inscribe this moment in my own.

The lurid sun behind
daubs the Long Walk houses
in an unearthly glow.
Boats are already tied
averting a clash

with a phalanx of foam.
Not much time left
to make a dash for home.
Sky opens like the sixth seal
this Galway afternoon.

A MOTHER NOW
for Lee

A mother now,
with Sudocrem behind my nails,
spare soothers in my purse,
nappies, wipes and Milton
on my perma-shopping list;
I measure hours in formula scoops,
have aged five years in five months.

A mother now,
I have books unread, plates unwashed,
floors unmopped, clothes heaped up,
teething rings in the fridge,
teats sterilizing by the sink.
I'm a sitting duck, feeding all day
with too much time to think.

A mother now,
there is purée in my freezer,
milky spittle on my shoulder.
eye pulses from lack of sleep,
mind swirls with tv themes.
I worry about brain atrophy
as I change the umpteenth nappy.
In a parallel universe, I'm reading theory.

A mother now,
my furniture's dented, beads are scattered,
some of my dreams are curdled.
I'm the same age as Lucy Jordan,
but unlike her, I have no desire
to 'ride through Paris in a sports car
with the warm wind in my hair'.

Your mother now,
each response to your new world
leaves you searching for answers in my face.
Your squeals of mirth illumine my day.
I thank you for this grace.

MUMMY FANTASIA

i Prams on the Prom

Sunday on Salthill promenade:
we are out with our babes,
high-tech push chairs on parade.
Your pram pivots round
on shock-absorber wheels
as you display its gadgetry:
USB port, cable for phone,
holders for sippy cups
and skinny lattes,
built-in generator
that charges as you walk.
'Never mind the Origami',
another mum exclaims,
'mine has a custom-built MP3 player,
hairdryer and cocktail mixer'.
You're pushing with one hand,
shaking with the other.
'Make mine a mojito!'
I holler, looking round
for the improbable stroller
with a waffle maker.

ii School Run Fashionistas

When did the school run
enter the style lexicon
as a plausible *mise-en-scène*?
Fashion-forward mums
teeter on heels,
pour coins in parking meters,
accoutred in Armani,
toting Gucci, cascading wipes

from couture catsuits.
They throw appraising glances
at other designer-clad mummies,
rain and wind buffeted
in Vivienne Westwood,
leaking indiscretions at school gates,
bantering in Blahniks, channeling Versace.

Magazines market with phrases:
'there's no excuse to be a slummy mummy'.
Should we take them quite so seriously?

DAMNED IF YOU DO …

Still learning the grammar
of being a mother;
'What is baby's centile?
How are you going
with tummy time?'
Do I hide that bottle of formula
now you're no longer breastfeeding?
Do eyes glower in reproof
as I gently get your wind up
at my mums' group?

'You're returning to work?
I would never leave mine in care
for more than one day –
not when they're so small!'

I zig zag your stroller
through tutting mothers,
catch the knowing smile
of others, jerking
back wheels away
from aphorisms of
Chinese Tiger matriarchs;
laissez-faire mamans.

I am literate in love; fluent in
fluids, weaning and nurture.
Time to throw away the primers.
My darling, you and I
will learn by trial and error.

ICE FLOWERS

Christmas day, feet crunch into snow
past drooping trees, touched by recurrence
of a geometric mystery. When hands
are mottled by cold, seeping into bone, I turn
back, understanding happiness has changed.
Lattices on a pane of father's car
are ferns dilating from a whole. We are
fractals: six sides of an ice crystal.
As a child, these days grew familiar
after greetings, stories, cups of tea.
Now among parents, sisters, children
our laughing boy kindles Christmas.
The wonder of each ice flower:
joy blooms in repetition.

LASSITUDE

Drooped on the couch
reading about raves,
the pursuit of the muse
in underground culture,
I feel my clinical label:
'geriatric mother'.

Baby woke just after ten,
teetered, tottered, toppled cds,
ripped everything off the table;
decreed to play until 3am.
Energy is bankrupt
from this sleep deficit
as I try to make the leap beyond
the ambit of the armrest.

Motherhood has numbed
what was once defined.
Lolling in the maelstrom,
I wonder what might happen
if I should also choose
to throw an artistic tantrum?

That would be a dereliction –
nothing would get done.
Our sitting room's a litter bin:
Tori Amos
is missing in the chaos
I am the jaded Fisher King,
trailing my grail through thick and thin.

Virginia Woolf wouldn't be pleased
I've a room of my own
that never gets used.

Roland Barthes, did you dare to utter
one cannot be both writer and mother?
Yes, I guess, it's death to the author.

Is superwoman really a myth?
How do bleary mums get through this?
Must I abandon creating
now I'm curator of the bottle steriliser,
more *hausfrau* than high brow?

'When you're up to your neck
in excrement',
Beckett said,
'all you can do is laugh'.
Vanilla Ice has come on 'Hi-5'
and, swaddling my son,
we dance around
to 'Ice-Ice Baby':
our final demolition.

LAMENT FOR LONG-LOST SUNDAY ROASTS

No excuse to use a mallet,
    (her husband eats no meat),
the best she can do,
    is tenderise tofu
with the pounding staccato
    of her wooden spoon.

SUSPENSION
Fr. Burke Park Playground, Galway

Sitting on a child's swing
in a mild trance of joy,
we lurch and listen for the hum
of our sing-song pendulum:
hee-haw-hee-haw
a kind of donkey metronome.
Thighs no longer feel the pinch
from the chunky chain links
as legs kick out and in.

The sun still gleams at seven.
My baby boy sits on my lap,
my arm fused to his waist.
His crown nestles under my chin,
eyes beam up at mine,
thrilling to our swoop and rise:
hee-haw-hee-haw,
pointing to a white arc,
faint in our blue sky.

'Moon!' his favourite word,
he repeatedly exclaims.
I wish I could freeze our frame,
swaying languidly
across the azure
keeping the easy tempo:
hee-haw-hee-haw
so I shut my eyes,
imprint it on my lids;
we are forever stilled
until the clang of a recorded bell
sunders our floating spell,
breaks our lunar reverie.

TÓRAÍOCHT

You dreamt of the thread count
of the sheets on our bed
in our adopted land;
rooms of deep colours,
paradisial quiet,
bathed in golden sunshine.

Now we lie in our *leaba síoda*,
I am Gráinne, you are Diarmuid,
under rich seams of earth,
between finely woven fibres;
everything is in reverse
after jumping hemispheres.

We find ourselves at the interstice
of the summer and winter solstice.
Have traded long daylight hours
for crisp, abrupt sunsets.

But this shift brings its own largesse
in a netherworld of naked branches,
airless gaps between skyscrapers,
where the city holds its breath.

The crescent moon hangs
in a promising smile
above our new horizon line,
touching fields of vision
as we unmoor our minds,
wait for cargo to arrive.

We are not exiles, we will return,
happy wherever we beach.
Because home is a concept, like a grail.

Another climate, another season,
after upheaval of leaving
family and possession.

We have creased that king-sized sheet
but ours is a lasting fabric
with no need for the monolithic
between Asia and the Antarctic.
We have filaments to swathe
each mutual dream and longing.

ANAM CARA
for Kevin

The universe was kind in the end,
though we waited decades
for our story to begin.

Now you are written
in my bloodstream;
a lark soaring through
the circadian zone
of my night owl.

I grow warm inside
when I spy your chartreuse
scarf we joked about,
billowing jauntily
like a Chinese dragon.

We snaked through
serpentine Marrakech:
two breathless children
on the trail of tassles
to suspend from keys,
unlock the ordinary.

In Berlin, you reclaimed
our smirched linden leaves
to place them under a frame.

I want to give you a lifetime
of lime blossom and rose water
and thereafter, if I have to choose,
because of our differing creeds,

I would rather loaf in limbo
for eternity, with you,
than toddle to paradise
on my own.

MUSICA UNIVERSALIS

On a lucid night,
as my street dreams,
I'm an antenna
attuned to an ancient
silence.

A sad note spirals
from the spheres;
though I am not Pythagoras.
I think of starlight yet
to reach us, and abstruse
nebulae moving farther
away.

A Copernicus I knew,
who made the earth move,
is now a speck of dust.

Will we ever know
what dark matter
disturbed the orbit
of our harmony?

I have seen the night sky
in the Southern Hemisphere,
memories of familiar
clusters disappear.

Once we scored
a universe; conducted
glinting staves,
oblivious
to dewy grass.

Eons and revolutions;
muted nocturnes
between us.

Frequencies found
in symphonic
stillness.

BRADÁN FEASA DEARMADTA

Seanfhocal: Éist le fuaim na habhann
agus gheobhaidh tú breac.

Tá bradáin ag streacailt
   sa bhFeoir i gCill Chainnigh,
léimeann said agus teipeann orthu.
   Tá an bradán feasa ar sheachrán fada
chun teacht slán san Éire nua.
   Tá ardmheas Finégas ar lár.
An bhfuil ár linn-ne ag dul amú
   gan éisteacht leis na héisc?
Tá na coraí ró-ard
   is gheobhaidh said bás
muna n-éisteann muid arís
   le síorfhuaim na habhann.

SOME DAY I MAY BE 'AUNTY EM'

Sporting a wicker hat
with assorted plastic fruit on top.
I may be that cycloptic aunt
with one eye ever magnified,
making sense of footnotes
that carry me off
to a precise world.

Or I may be that aunt
referred to as a vamp,
rocking black leather pants,
recalling Blondie and Chrissie Hynde
who left punk men behind,
living it up and kicking it live
with a younger generation
who see me as a grand-dame type
Marianne Faithfull,
unfazed by alienation,
laughing in the face of women
who think I should know better.

No More Nomads

I've met my share
of angry poets,
slippery hippies
in the garb of liberals;
mellow and flaky,
masters of reiki,
stubbing out visions
in empty beer cans.

Lefty values dreadlocked
in undefined fare
of pacifists with clotted hair
juggling liberties on Eyre Square;
swirling diabolos by arches;
neither Gothic or Romanesque
but flying buttresses
for a woolly wonderland
where no one takes a stand.

This is no 'graveyard of ambition'.
I will lock away my kaftan,
fasten my tie-dye dress to the collar,
vow to deflect attentions
of beguiling knaves, raffish ravers,
firebrands, freeloaders,
shitehawkers, interlopers.

Am I prone to fripperies
of bohemian stragglers;
musical swagger
of raggle-taggle dawdlers
capering in corners?
Enough imbroglios
with louche lotharios,

arching pierced brows
between jigs 'n' reels,
drum 'n' bass,
banter and palaver.

Don't get me wrong –
I respect those hangers-on;
who find themselves marooned
in the last chance saloon,
cadging warmth from nicotine,
but there are colts in clouds all about me.

ROCKS AND SOFT PLACES

Behind the counter
of a gemstone jeweller
I preside over turquoise.

Crystals cluster about me,
willing me to know their names:
azurite, tourmaline, peridot.

I am a magpie:
jasper, topaz, tiger's eye.
I am guardian
of a semi-precious hoard:
amethyst, malachite, moonstone.

Lamps and mirrors catch facets
of sapphire amulets,
blue scintilla of labradorite,
mossy thread of dendrite.

Windows are adorned
with showpiece torcs,
festooned with fluorite,
smoky quartz.

My dreams are latticed
with blue lace agate –
crusted with rocks,
tumbled and polished;
minerals deeply deposited.

Gems regale me with
each fissure and inclusion,
impel me to trace their veins
of heat and diffusion.

I wish I could believe
in their subtle vibrations:
rose quartz to attract true love,
amber to cleanse the chakras,
gold-specked lapis lazuli
to open the third eye.

COCOON

I thought I came unstuck
a long time ago,
but still I find bits of larva
in my clothes and hair
each passing year;
pupa dreams entangled
in slimy film, their images
flicker against the screen
of this silky membrane,
like the fragile beating
of fledgling wings
jostling with hardening time.

Do I cling to my empty shell
or does it cleave to me?
Sometimes it is my proscenium
and I am on stage again,
waiting for my curtain call –
was I ever fledged at all?
The temptation to retreat
into the world within
this casing I have spun
is a constant pull.
It seems I'm half a caterpillar
in a greenroom that is windowless.
Where is the dream fulfiller?

I have glimpsed
the beauty of my wings,
not their symmetric lineaments.
Before I had a chance to flee
a web of stasis
closed in around me.
But my spirit politely

refuses to be ushered
fully from this chrysalis
until ready to flutter.

EKPHRASIS: WEAVER IN AFGHANISTAN
on viewing a photographic exhibition by Mike Bunn

Lines of natural fibre
weave the fabric
worn for centuries.
Dyes of walnut, apricot,
onion skins
have not changed,
nor the looms or spinning wheels
that dwell behind
the 'hidden paradise'
of the Hindukush valley
where no mountain
is a mountain
till it reaches 15,000 feet.

In that free-running spool,
an elision of memory:
spinning and carding,
layering all sadness,
laughter, sickness, struggle.
Lines on your face work placidly
into the web of the *shu*,
and you, valued member
of your mountain village,
weave a lifetime,
knowing it's in the teasing out
that we are all the same.

BLIND SPOTS

Everyone has their own scotoma.
Even Newton toyed with alchemy.
The great vivisector, Aristotle,
toppled by the common eel.
Heidegger clung to fascism;
Schopenhauer to sexism.
Sackville-West believed
the Nile flowed backward.
I hope my own conviction
is not my Achilles heel.

Rap Riposte

You urge me to write
of that grittier life –
some dirty realist doggerel
of doggone streets of grime,
tie a tourniquet round my arm,
shoot up with anti-anodyne.

Do I fall from grace
to save literary face;
some kind of sacrifical virgin
enrolled in a junkie bedsit
just to get a taste of it?

Sorry to disappoint,
I'll never burn a spoon.
But I don't do *bourgeois* rhyme.

I am a logophile
where words take flight
through musicality,
mimetic capability,
image rendered vividly,
or simply a design
upon a naked page.

I'm an upbeat poet –
get-over-it!; not in
thrall to tortured artists,
black-wearing apologists.
Though I keep my eyes open,
I will never proselytise. This
is my bird-flipping diatribe
from the city of the tribes:

if literary truth be told
your words of gritty woe
are just the argot
of another orthodoxy

Club Oa2

Dhá roth móra
os mo chomhair
slua súgach,
leathólta
ag leanúint a n-anama
is a gcosa.
Sac mór cheirníní
lán le gheallúintí

Cén fáth go bhfuilim anseo?

Toisc gurb aoibhinn linn an ceol
mar go bhfuil faoiseamh ó dhaoine
mar go bhfaighim féin faoiseamh
as aoibhneas na rithime.

Mothaím an gliondar
ag ardú ionam
pobal lastiar díom
do mo thionlacan
ag ceiliúradh is ag cur fúthu
ar phláinéad an urláir.

Géilleann muid don draíocht,
éalaíonn an fhilíocht.
Braithimid aontas na daonnachta
i rithimí teo cheoil dhomhanda.

Seo anois mo fhreagrachtsa
féachaint chuig ardú meanman.

Dhá roth móra
os mo chomhair

ag síorchasadh nuacheoil na cruinne
do phobal na Gaeilge
pobal an uile dhuine.

Agus sé mana an tslua ag an deireadh
ná 'tiúin amháin eile, tiúin amháin eile!'

ODE TO LOST POEMS

I am standing at the precipice
    of something ludicrous:
leaning over the half-door
    of conscious and unconscious;
the thrill of the original
    jolts my solar plexus.

Calliope waves her stylus
    over my hypothalamus,
ignites synapses
    with new hypotheses,
admts me into ontologies
    of things foreign to me.

Alphabets reorder themselves
    into hieroglyphs and ideograms,
the cosmic Chain of Being
    is just as Dante divines:
we hover in between
    angels and animals.

Da Vinci's Vitruvian man
    cartwheels through my dreams,
bears me back to ancient Greece:
    I am Aspasia, holding court
at my symposia, arguing
    with Socrates for marital parity.

He spins and vaults again:
    now I am Artemisia,
trying to impress my talents
    upon phallocentric Florence ...

I am the Sibyl at Delphi,
    prophesying in a heated frenzy
that echos for millennia.

But, unwilling to shed this sleep,
    I toss and turn sluggishly
lolling on a mattress of poems
    from each phase of my life:
some seeped into its foam;
    others were caught in time.

OIDHREACHT

My Irish dreamtime
is Clarke's 'Lost Heifer',
the drone of a piper,
planxties of a harper,
sweaty ceillís at fleadh ceoils;
raw beauty of the natural world;
bards nostalgic for a Gaelic order.

I prefer the honesty of Kavanagh
buoyed by the spiritual,
to the affectation of Yeats,
whose elegance I appreciate.
And that defining moment
in Irish poetry
was Hartnett's decision
to relinquish English,
return to *an Ghaeilge.*

I hear the resonance
of Bunting's collections
in Moore's permutations,
cadences of 'The Nation',
Duanaire of the dispossessed;
echoes of my ancestors
who clung to their faith
as a stronghold of hope,
and the Congress of 1932
captured by Cartier Bresson
viewed at a gallery in Brussels:
tweed-capped men down on their knees,
dotted for miles on Irish bóithríns.

I think of our penal cross,
the lure of the Mass Rock,

and Brian Ó Laoí,
swapping his clothes
for the priest's robe,
in the Glen of Aherlow
at the sound of the horses
of the red coats.

Still perplexed, I'm carried
by my Grandmother's conviction
echoing, proudly, up from our kitchen:
'Faith of our fathers, holy faith'.

TIME OF YOUR BIRTH
for Lee

You were born into love
in a time of tumult:
Arab Spring in Egypt,
civil war in Libya,
tsunami in Japan.

The harp your mother played
hangs in mercantile gaze
on the National Asset
Management Agency;
its strings jarringly pulled
to bail out bankers' bonds.

They thought 'boom' meant progress,
not a loud, plangent note
booming through escheated estates,
vacant and desolate.

Our debt clock is ticking
at over one hundred billion.
Time and tide are in arrears.
On everyone's lips:
the levy we're bequeathing
to our children and their offspring.

On streets of Athens,
Greeks are shouting;
we're not like the Irish –
we will keep on fighting.
In ancient cairns
the *Fianna* lie sleeping.

May your brilliant light
flare through the grey severity
of a country beleaguered
by its economy.
May you value your heritage
and never
submit.

IN MEMORY OF MY GRANDMOTHER
Eileen Lee née Brosnan (1920–2009)
'To unlock a society, look at its untranslatable words'
– Salman Rushdie

Your words were windows on a Gaelic world –
unofficial *seanchaí* of our family.
Your similes and phrases,
novel and spontaneous,
about 'cows not finding
their calves in this mess',
the 'happiness of a cow
and a cock of hay'.

You knew all the ballads of Thomas Davis,
fused Gaelic words with English phrases:
óinseach, sagosha, tháfhéalan;
sang old comeallyas
while baking tarts,
told stories of bringing
your cart to the creamery,
piglets to the mart
when a single girl in Brosna.
You wrote to query de Valera;
he praised your self-reliance.

You spotted Granda,
waiting for confession.
His piety and uniform
made an impression.
He followed your
brown eyes to England
to ask for your hand.

Gregory Peck noticed your raven hair
when he waltzed you from the crowd

in Kerry, in 1956
while filming *Moby Dick*.

You taught me the Holy Spirit prayer:
'Soul of my soul I adore thee',
introduced me to Sister Faustina
and the Divine Mercy.
I bear witness to your transmission
of faith, folklore, tradition.
May we hear your voice at the threshold again,
bidding us 'Welcome, Welcome,
Welcome'.

HOLIDAY PIANO

Ivories were foxed and worn
like sun-faded paper,
not lacquered like our own.
Pedals were a little stiff but
sound could be as loud, if
less subtle – *pianissmo*
was barely possible
so I belted out songs
my aunty left behind:

'Morning has Broken', a youthful
Cat Stevens on the cover,
Elton John's 'Crocodile Rock'.

I danced like a crustacean
to stun relations: chromatic
crawls over
octaves.

Less the baby grand,
more the feisty refrain
of a honky-tonk bar,
it had long since seen
a tuner but
had the same power
to hold the moment;
didn't have to be
in concert pitch;
all that had to be done
transposed by

no-school days with cousins,
bacon and turnips, pails
of fresh milk with apple tarts.

It vibrated through my
grandmother's home,
sustained
the pitch
of her hearth.

GAISCE CLAIRSEORA

Bhí amhras ar Art Mac Murrow
é ag marcaíocht i dtreo an fhéasta
ach ba dheas an cuireadh a fháil
ó na Tiarnaí Sasanacha laistigh den Pháil.

Suíonn sé ag an mbord flaithiúil
is casann i dtreo a chláirseora:

'Chun mo bhuíochas a léiriú díbh
is cóir ceiliúradh le ceol na cláirsí.
Ar aghaidh leat, a fhir mhaith,
cas port binn d'fhadsaol ár dTiarnaí'.

Tagann faitíos ar aghaidh an cheoltóra;
tugann sé rud aisteach faoi ndeara:
tá airm i lámha na saighdiúirí –
ní haíonna iad ach príosúnaigh!

Tarraingíonn sé na sreanganna
bo tréan is go géar –
in ionad geantraí a chasadh
seinneann sé Rosc Catha.

Tá fearg ar Art Mac Murrow:
níl said ag troid ach ag ithe!
Cén fáth go bhfuil cláirseoir
chomh mímhúinte seo
ina fhostaíocht aige?
Tugann sé íde béile dá fhear
ach leanann sé leis an Rosc Catha.

Tá an dearg-ghoimh ar Mac Murrow anois,
ní fhaigheann sé nod mo dhuine.

Éiríonn sé lena chluasa a bhualadh
ach, mo lean, céard a nochtar sa nóiméad san?

Feiceann sé gléasanna na dTiarnaí
is tuigeanna go raibh sé le láimhsiú.
Rabhadh mór a bhí sa cheol –
ní mór dóibh éalú láithreach.

Beireann sé greim ar a chláirseoir
is léimeann said suas ar a gcapaill.
Is mar sin a shábháil cláirseoir cróga
saol Airt Mhic Mhurrow.

GOOGLE EARTHED

In memory of poet, Patrick Kavanagh (1904–1967),
who held that the parochial was universal

When we guide satellite pictures
from our sitting-room
to delineate our street,
we are deities
morphing aerial maps
into faultlines and heartlines.

As we bond over the globe,
our Parnassian love, giddy
with promises of technology,
raises us to omnipotence.

I think of all the topographies
you have shown me,
places pin-dropped to visit:
from the stark Atlas Mountains
to the geysers of Iceland.

We zoom out again
to the curvature of Earth,
and the parochial
becomes universal
under our right-click,
sturdy hawthorn stick.
I muse that Patrick Kavanagh
might have parted
with his beloved bicycle
for this momentary epic.

BACKING UP

Streaming music constantly,
your face firewalls me.
You can barely interact
for loading MP3s.

'You should be syncing all the time',
you chide, with each new ping.
I'm a child scorned,
dumber than my smartphone.

Like some kind of ancient prophet,
you let me scroll your tablet.
How could you know
I crave a calf-bound folio?

I do not share your viral buzz,
but dream of going analog again,
scrawling virgin-white paper
in rolls of my fountain pen.

When did you rewire our code?
You think I commit the cardinal sin
of not backing up everything
while our memories go up into clouds.

COMPILATION TAPE

'Thank you for the days':
the song you proffered, graciously,
as our contact ceased.

A soundtrack mapped by you
prompted a craze in me
for earmarking inner galaxies,

labelling each one lovingly,
cutting out an apposite
graphic for its inlay.

Sometimes your tape
got caught from overplay –
I would stick a biro in the spool,

wind our chart back into place,
marshal into a kind of order
soundscapes I could not control.

Time has spliced them apart,
but my impulse to fossilize emotion
into musical impressions

– neat, rectangular artifacts –
has never been replaced
by new audio formats.

I recall the joy they brought:
those peerless lo-fidelity
musical *mappae mundis*.

GOOGLED

I google your name;
and a baby's head in Arizona;
a thirty-something
professional runner;
an elder lemon academic
discoursing in
Wyoming,

are thumbnails
I blow up full-size.
Perversely, I long
for some clue
as to where you have moved,

until pixel by pixel
your face mosaics
into my bit bucket,
defying the fibre-optic coil.
I sit, fully self-aware
of my stubbornness to remain alone
in my Platonic cyber-cave
where memory is virtually
dredged; all constructed
as its image.

On Attending the Cúirt Festival of Literature

Flushed into daylight,
I leave the Town Hall
goose-pimpled,
replaying images.

Eleven am is early
for poetry, they say.
Words orbit,
still sinking in,
as I saunter to the Salmon Weir
in a shock of cool, midday air.

I replay their sounds in my mind
as a cormorant swoops for fish.
Stopping to guess when he'll surface again,
I will him to bring something up.

A pause, then he reappears.
Tropes begin to ring
clear.
I cross the street while he passes beneath
to emerge with a trout in his yellow beak.

As he grasps his prize,
metaphors speak.

ARS MUSICA

If I were to score
the syncopation
of our relationship
there would be semi-quavers,
truncated harmonics,
plaintive semibrieves.
Reverberating silence –
a *glissando* of high drama –
some fluid viola moments
counterpointed
by an unruly zylophone
running away
with itself.

THE R & J LETTER*

Taki, your missives are tacky
and your mistresses are lacking.
Word is getting round
that your template love letters
are quoting Shakespeare
to put the come-hithers
on literary ditzes,
and American cultural tourists.

Replicating Romeo:
'But heaven's here, where Juliet lives',
somehow virgins fall for it.
It only takes one glance to spawn
your ready-made parlance.
Each Juliet of the moment
believes she alone inspired it
and you are known
as 'best lover of the Western World'.

Now *Spectator* readers
are unwittingly treated
to your ersatz *belle-lettres*
in a public confession!
All those *ingénues*
who accommodated you
taken in by the ruse
of your *billet-doux*.

What bewilders me
is how a man can get away
with such unoriginality.

* English writer, Taki, known for his amorous skillfulness, created the following template love letter, which he repeatedly issued to the object of his desire as if he had just composed it spontaneously:

"Dear X,
There's a marvellous line in Romeo & Juliet when Romeo – having arranged Mercutio's death – is advised to flee Verona. 'But Heaven's here where Juliet lives', he cries. However corny and sudden this may sound, this is how I felt since the moment I met you. Love Taki"

JOWL

What shall I do with this body they gave me,
so much my own, so intimate with me?

– Osip Mandelstam

Your lipstick meanders
outside the line of your thinning lips.
You leave the house in your current state,
abandon your eyeliner flick;
your come-to-bed eyes
never-got-to-bed eyes.

Everyone knows a woman must
maintain her youthful good looks.

'Muscle has memory', you tell yourself,
panting on the treadmill,
willing your thighs to remember
they were flagrantly slimmer.
Are you two dress sizes
from happiness?
At least you feel no pressure
to schedule a vajazzle.

Everyone knows a woman must
maintain her youthful good looks.

You blend foundation into
changing contours of your face,
wondering when exactly
your pores became craters.
Blusher is your best friend
now you're blanched
like a bunch of asparagus spears.

Everyone knows a woman must
maintain her youthful good looks.

Will you ever reclaim that alchemy
when your dress expressed you perfectly?
Your jokes were funnier, your hair glossier:
your tresses billowed – now they're flyaway.
You moved with *élan* on the dancefloor,
trod lightly, didn't spill gravy.

Everyone knows a woman must
maintain her youthful good looks.

You will grow old gracefully
except grace is a myth;
the world ignores women
who slide into invisibility.
They already start to cut you off,
in pre-emptive glances at a watch.
So pop open the serum and primer,
remember to drink ten gallons of water,
learn how to be *soignée*
or choose opacity.

Because everyone knows a woman must
maintain her youthful good looks.

You who were always diffident
about the male gaze,
who never suspected those catcalls
were directed toward you,
can enjoy keeping your thoughts intact;
no worries about being leered at,
nurture what is hidden,
focus on seeing anew.

Screw you.

for the sake of *Sex and the City*,
an act few writers could excuse
but it satisfied entirely!
I sat there, let them fade
away: ideas and associations,
novel rhyme formations
and could I care less?
No – vapours dispersed.
I sank down deeper and deeper
in my non-metaphorical sofa.

Have I broken
some time-honoured code –
the primacy of the word?
Or should I just accept
that now I'm up to date
with the dating lives
of four New Yorkers?
Should I relish this departure
or question the impulse
for pleasures so temporal?
Think of Flaubert, the true ascetic,
grafting alone in his freezing attic!

Are those the voices
of Keats and Shelley
censuring my love of telly?
On the contrary,
they rejoice for me.
I have broken the bondage
of documentation,
the implicit mechanism
of literary narcissism.

Tonight I was right
for once, to indulge.
Maybe one day
I'll redress lacunae:
Samantha's demeanour
will yield a steamy sestina.

GALWAY MOULD

We take the damp for granted here.
Blinds draw back to reveal
colonies of galaxies:
tiny black holes
in our new collective space.

'It's only condensation',
Next Door concedes,
'the weather's too wintry
to open the windows'.
My wooden bangle by the sill
slips into a mildewed coat of green.

For fun, I bought you mouldy cheese.
Last night, it took revenge on me,
inducing a vivid dream
of a white chandelier of mould
that slowly lowered
through our kitchen ceiling:
a lichen lantern,
till its lattices became milky spores,
mouths that started to open and close.

Then I awoke, vowing to spray
our wall of condensation,
diffuse for good my fascination
with Galway mould.

LETTING GO OF LANGUAGE

The rest of this must be said in silence
Because of the enormous difference between light
And words that try to say light
– from 'A Cleared Site' by Rumi, trans. Coleman Barks

Walking toward the Atlantic,
absent-minded,
force of habit;
to shake off the day
heat surges to my fingers –
tips become lit tapers.

Jolted by the sunset:
a proud, majestic ember
in a grate of ashes,
it flares one final expanse
of a penumbral sky.

My body fathoms
words fall flat. every phrase
I've ever learnt
can't capture that contrast

so I just let it smoulder
in my pockets;
trundle home,
a firmament
consuming my back.

COFFEE TABLE

A sigh of relief:
the coffee table's clean.
Gone are bills, bank statements,
that half Liga biscuit,
spattering of raisins.
If it's even partly clutter-free,
I can hear myself think again.
How did I end up
taking such delight
in a small, sovereign surface?
Once a dark wood cot,
now remade with sheet of glass
into this low centre-piece.
I assess its patina and ask:

Have my days become
a series of small wins
from routine chores
ticked off to-do lists?
Yes, perhaps, but there is joy
in striking through,
winning that extra hour
while a baby sleeps.

I bless scuff marks,
avert shiny rings
left over from hot drinks
as I burnish smirches
of grime, yet feel a pang
for squandered time
congeal like a blob
of baby cereal.

This is how it feels:
content for now
as wife and mother,
here on leave from
over-arching deadlines,
targets, protracted career goals,
presentations long carried over
and I cannot help but wonder if
this kempt coffee table
is the cradle of my peace of mind.

Just Before Sleep
Vision after feeding my baby

I lie on a bed of memories; upon rich, fertile loam.
Some of the seeds that took were knowingly sown.

Many, carried by the wind, seeded by chance.
I tended some, the rest relied on rain and sun;

I wish I had green fingers so I could have known
which were perennial. New shoots furl around

my head, burst forth in vivid colour. Others
bloom into flowerless fronds with phantom

spores that tickle my nose. Faces from my past
float aloft stalks. Have my hands grown any wiser?

Languid in my raised bed, I'm no longer entangled
in a thicket of bramble. I deadhead drooping tendrils,

yet, I have also learned to live with wild accretion,
trust sequestered bulbs through a phlegmatic winter.

AUGENBLICK (BLINK OF AN EYE)

An evening walk
by the bay with pram,
he is feisty, mid-tantrum.
Flagging in the Antarctic wind,
you are clammy, chagrined.
A dusky sky is shot through
with snatches of a distant past.

Vague yearnings, long suppressed,
bob on the surface of upswell;
jetsam
barely noticed
before it is washed away again.

A wasp hovers
by his sticky arm.
Your rapid swivel, a familiar giggle,
wings battle a truck's tail-wind.
Hilarity of this new game.

In a second
you record the spectres,
then let montages fade;

turn away
from the vanishing curve
of a ghostly galleon.

Whatever is lost is tossed
to sea. Possibilities
glimmer on the horizon.

BREAKING OUT IN THE KITCHEN

I am a starlet *manqué*,
can pout and dance in perfect time
with whatever rhythm you throw at me.
My mind is alert, body relaxed,
in perfect syntax with the universe ...

Holding a bowl of puréed mash,
in a groove, light fantastic,
I shimmy to Sister Sledge
who have just come on the radio:

'We're lost in music,
feel so alive, I quit
my nine-to-five
we're lost in music'.
I want to sing, in high decibels:
'I'm fully alive and whimsical!'

My ten month-old
laughs in hilarity
from his high chair,
thrilling to the lilt
as I shake my hair.

We are having a moment,
not *Dancing at Lughnasa* -
more like dancing lunacy,
with the same spontaneity.

The song ends and,
as he claps his tiny hands,
in the privacy of our kitchen
on a stark, Monday afternoon,
I recognise a fan for life.

AMARYLLIS

You raced round the city
to buy flowers for our guest.
We three sat drinking tea,
willing bulbs to sprout,
but last night she had to leave
before their world unfolded.

The amaryllis amplify
how it feels to be loved by you
from the inside out.

I enter the kitchen to behold
their inflorescence.
Morning light floods in
upon the table
where two proud stalks
are gallant sentinels.
Bewitched, I touch their
carmine red trefoils,
blooms of burnished wax.

Soon they will be pendulous,
shedding one by one.
But I will remember
how they hold their elative heads
on a stark december morning;
their sturdy elegance
irradiating everything.

GALWAY FLUX

i Saturday Afternoon

Ozone and olive oil marinate an Atlantic breeze;
brine and garlic meander from the market.

Salmon skirt waders, crossing the weir;
we spy a Galway hooker, dawdling at the pier.

Students are Buckfastened by sluggish canals,
buskers belt out ballads:

'I'll tell me ma when I go home
the boys won't leave the girls alone'.

Revellers swig cider in Wellingtons
bounding to a gig at Leisureland.

On Quay Street, a melodeon plays 'Drowsy Maggie';
a diva renders 'You Fill Up My Senses'.

Vibrato mingles with timbre of tourists
babbling outside restaurants.

ii Saturday Evening

Teeming mist and ocean spray
are Venus rising from the waves,

alighting from an oyster shell
borne on the ebb of Atlantic swell

entering the bay from some mellow canal
whose only competition: the regal heron

down river where 'Anach Cuan'
followed the drowning of Menlo;

Galvia outruns Anna Livia
in sluicing, runneling pinnacle

stone-age halberds exhumed in the silt,
remains of a grandiose railway bridge.

And in this infinite maritime:
the salt-aired flux of Galway.

MACASAMHAIL

Is tú mo mhacasamhail:
mac mo shamhlaíochta,
macalla mo shamhailteacha.

A chomhthaistealaí,
cuireann tú ina luí
ar m'intinn
gur féidir mo scíth
a ligint
is beidh réiteach
ar gach scéal,
faoiseamh
ó chuile imní.

Cothaíonn muid
tearmann croí
ar scáth a chéile,
faoi anáil an duine eile,
is bláthaím i ndídean
do ghlóir is do ghéaga,

ceann scríbe m'anama.

CROSS-POLLENATORS

i

He keeps a paintbrush
in the peak of his cap
as he does the work of the bees.
Strolling round his estate,
he removes corolla,
brushes stigma,
paints pollen onto stamen.
Dreaming of new phenomena,
he admires his multi-coloured flora,
whispers unorthodox prayers
for fields of hybrid flowers.

ii

Each spring, with a matchstick
behind his ear,
he skewers half a Rooster
with half a Kerr Pink,
buries it carefully in the earth
where pests won't get at it.
Four months later
his flowery potato
becomes his thrill
in nudging nature.

FLIGHT PATHS
for my sister, Benita

We stall in a rose garden,
on a balmy afternoon,
by rambling polyantha beds
in their first bloom.
Soft amplitude
suffuses the space
between words spoken
and unsaid.

A foghorn and a jet
sound at the same time.
You say you don't mind
how flight paths change,
a bit of noise now and then
is not too much to pay
to live so close to Dublin Bay.

I snap you among crimson
blossoms at their peak,
awed by what you will undertake,
surprised by your ease, calm
insight; my hand, tentatively
on your taut belly –
each of us on her own trajectory.
I hold this precious confluence.

PRIMAVERA

That feeling when spring
spikes your bloodstream;

fresh eddies of air, caressing,
in breezy street-crossings.

You are treading lightly,
everything is syncing;

buoyancy you can't deny
breaks through resignation.

Mosaics of colour
cleave your *anomie*

as buds return to bushes
with a new effervescence.

You are alive,
incandescent,

alert to species,
ideas seeding,

the future, wide open,
beginning here.

INDEFINITE DESIRE

I want to eat something
I cannot quite place;
nothing clichéd
like a crumbling Flake
while I lie supine in a tub
like the Lady of Shalott.
No need to phone down
for Imperial Leather, Jeeves.
I'm still searching for
those kaffir lime leaves,
questing for a seasoning
just right for me.

Among crisp husks
and burst membranes
my taste buds seethe
for a marinade
beyond the media pedlars;
not a tangy pomegranate
I lasciviously suck,
(though the fruits of the male gaze
are difficult to purge).

As the winter nights draw in
I find myself ladling
turmeric, cumin,
quills of cinnamon,
musky nutmeg
pungent okar –
I pomander oranges
with cloves;
could not live
without coriander,
the perfume of pasta

reeking with basil,
curry redolent
with garam masala.

I will make sweetmeats
with pods of vanilla,
threads of saffron, quinces,
pinches of cardamom,
bittersweet cocoa,
sensing I'm getting closer
to the fragrant bouquet
of a quenching aroma.

PLAYING HOUSE

Today I'm in between
the wall and the armrest
in a kind of intertext,
playing house with my son
while trying to set up
our real-life home.

After phoning the Good Guys
about delivery of a dryer,
I visit him beside the sofa
in our *mise-en-scène*,
he rings an imaginary bell
under the colonnades
of the kitchen table, where
we pipedream domesticity
in our newly-adopted city.

I feel like a figure from metafiction:
the *French Lieutenant's Woman*
or a reverie of Flann O'Brien
befuddled in the aisles
between slatted beds,
flat and fitted sheets
(Egyptian only fits a Single –
polycotton left for a Queen).

Even a toddler, not quite two,
manifests an edifice.
He grins with pride
at his brand new coup
of dragging the coffee table
from one end of the room,
while I run the gauntlet
to stop him flicking switches,

my head pondering over
the virtues of a condenser
or that cheaper top loader.

DOCTORED

I bind my thesis
    between solid covers,
        knowing words are not finite.

Scholars gloss footnotes in new *études,*
    but deep in academia
        there are no absolutes.

PALIMPSEST

You wonder if, sometimes,
we underrate our nation,
when you discover
your friend from Australia
has the Irish word for 'faith'
tattooed upon her back
in discreet Gaelic script.

On a crisp winter evening
at a tram stop in Melbourne,
she lifts her woollen sweater,
to reveal her deep imprint,
of the country and culture
where she worked and lived,
in a single word:
creideamh.

Emily Cullen is a writer, scholar, harpist and arts manager from Farney Castle, Co. Tipperary. A long-time Galway resident, she was the inaugural Arts Officer of NUI Galway between 1999 and 2002. Her first collection, entitled *No Vague Utopia*, was published by Ainnir in 2003. In 2004 she was the national Programme Director of the Patrick Kavanagh Centenary celebrations and was selected for the Poetry Ireland Introductions series. Emily was awarded an IRCHSS Government of Ireland fellowship for her doctoral study on the Irish harp. She is a qualified teacher of the harp who has performed throughout Europe, Australia and the United States. A former member of the Belfast Harp Orchestra, she has recorded on a number of albums and also as a solo artist. In addition to writing poetry, short stories and feature articles, she publishes widely on aspects of Irish cultural history and music. She currently works with the School of Arts and Sciences at the Australian Catholic University in Melbourne, Australia.